A collection of System Design Interview Questions

Antonio Gulli

System design is the ninth of a series of 25 Chapters devoted to algorithms, problem solving, and C++ programming.

DEDICATION

To Mimmo, my uncle. For inspiring my passion for technology

ACKNOWLEDGMENTS

Thanks to Dimitris Kouzis – Loukas for his Precious comments

Contents

Basic Knowledge

1. What are the important numbers to remember?

Solution

In preparation of a system design interview it could be useful to remind some measures about time, storage space, and networking.

TIME	
Sec	1
Msec	10^-3
Usec	10^-6
Nsec	10^-9

Data			
1Kbyte	10^3	2^10	
1Mbyte	10^6	2^20	
1Gbyte	10^9	2^30	2^32=4G
1Tbyte	10^12	2*60	2^64=16T
1Pbyte	10^15	2*120	

Please remember that it is not essential to memorize all the correct values for accessing a device (memory, storage, network) but it is certainly recommended to be aware of the order of magnitudes involved during the access. The following numbers are an average of what you get by using commodity servers.

Memory, Network, Disk	
Memory access	Nsec
Round trip same datacenter	Usec
Disk access	Msec

Memory access time is significantly impacted by the level of cache we are considering. An L1 cache is roughly speaking 10x faster than a L2 cache and 100x times faster than a DIMM memory. Again, here we are interested in the order of magnitudes and not necessarily in the actual values.

Memory	
L1 cache	1 nsec
L2 cache	10 nsec
Mem	100 nsec

Accessing a SATA disk can be 10.000 times slower than accessing memory. However, solid-state disks (SSD) can be 10x faster than a traditional disk (the distinction is mostly in terms of seek time as bandwidth is pretty much the same).

Disk	
Disk seek	10 msec
Read 1Mb	20 msec
Disk SSDs	0.1msec
Bandwidth	~30M/sec

Within a single datacenter, network latencies among servers can be much larger if they are located in different racks. Here, we assume that servers are connected with gigabit switches.

Rack server		Bandwidth
Same server	Mem: 100ns	20Gb/s
	Disk: 10ms	200M/sec
Same Rack	Mem: 300us	100M/sec
	Disk: 10ms	30Ms/sec
Different Rack	Mem:	10M/sec
	Disk:	10M/sec

The cost of a server can be impacted by many factors. In the following, there are some estimates for July 2016 with no particular discount applied. However it should be also mentioned that nowadays it is quite common to use a cloud-based solution. Amazon, Google, Microsoft and many others offer competitive solutions with always decreasing costs.

Having a good understanding of how much it will cost to establish a hardware platform is a prerequisite for many system design interviews. Therefore make sure that you have an updated picture before having the interview.

Cost of servers	2016
Intel 2Xeon quadcore	$900
Dimm 256Gb (32DIMM x 8GB)	$2000
Total 256GB ram only	**$2,5K-3K**
SSDs 1Tb	$500
Total with additional 24TB	**~$3K-3,5K**
8xSSDs 1Tb each = 8Tb	$2500-$3000
Total with disks and sdds	**~$6K**

QPS is the number of queries per second. Many factors can impact the results including the complexity of the data model adopted, where the data is located (memory, disk), the number of parallel clients, how complex queries are, hardware adopted and many other factors. The following numbers are indicative:

Some benchmark	These items are purely indicative as they depend on data, server configuration* and connections	
Memcached	200K-400Kqps	
Redis/Mongodb	100K-400Kqps	
Mysql	50K-100Kqps	

* Data based on a 2,5Ghz 8 core, 1Gbit Ethernet; all data in memory

Many system design interviews start with the so-called Fermi problems, where you need to estimate some values and make some back-of-the-envelope calculation. Again, it is not really important to know the exact values: what really matters is to have a ball-park guesstimate.

The following are some Internet stats for July 2016 including the number of Internet users, the number of Google queries, the number of

Facebook/Twitter active users per month, and some traffic related information.

Internet stats	2016
World inhabitants	7,5 billion
Internet users	3,5 billion
Email sent/day	131 billion (~20x Internet users)
Google queries/day	3,5 billion
Twitter post/day	400 Million
Youtube played videos/day	6,5 billion (~2x Internet users)
Youtube uploaded hours per minute	300 hours
Facebook mobile active users (MAU)	1,6 billion (~0.5x Internet users)
Facebook posts per minute	300K
Google+ MAU	500 Million
Internet Traffic	2B GB/day

2. What are the fundamental steps for system design interviews?

Solution

System design interviews are typically very interactive. Typically questions asked are quite open-ended and there is no exact solution. The interviewer is interested in understanding your communication and problem solving ability. The following four steps are minimal pre-requisite that is good to address during the interview:

1. Scope of the problem: think about different use cases and share them with the interviewer. Listen carefully to feedback since you don't want to start designing a system which is different from what is expected. Remember that interview questions are underspecified by design: the interviewer expects that you deal with uncertainty as it happens for all the situations in day-by-day work. Remember that

both your communications and your problem solving skills are tested.

2. Verify your requirements: think about important metrics for the problem. For instance, how many users will use the system, what is the storage space needed, how many queries per second we need to serve. This is the Fermi part where you might be requested to do also some back-of-the-envelope computation. Remember that you certainly need to address scalability, availability and consistency so certain trade-offs might be required. Again, make assumptions but share them with the interviewer: don't worry too much if you are off in some of the values as the interviewer is more interested in your way of thinking and (s)he will correct if you are off by a large amount. This does not mean that you don't need to know the order of magnitude required for accessing a disk (it's millisecond, see previous question) but it is ok if you don't remember the monthly active users in Facebook during last month. Remember that system design interviews are interactive.

3. Draw a high level abstract design: After scoping the problem, verifying the requirements and listening carefully the interviewer's feedback you can start drawing some high level abstract design on the white board separating the components in logical modules. It could be useful to identify what belongs to backend and what belongs to frontend. Explain how the customer will be served by your system. Still from a high level prospective describe what is your storage strategy, how data can be partitioned, where it could be useful to cache, how the backend is connected to the frontend, what level of parallelism is required for serving customers. Again, here you need to pay attention to the feedback of the interviewer and do not jump directly in describing every single module. First provide a horizontal high-level description that is consistent and elegant. Most likely the interviewer will ask you to describe more deeply one or two modules.

4. Discuss trade-offs: This is the most interesting part. Every single system design is about trade-offs. The following is a non-inclusive list of discussion points. Please note that we will address many of them in following questions:

a. You cannot have Consistency, Availability and (data) Partition at the same time so you need to trade one of them (do you know that Facebook, Amazon and many other run with eventual consistency? Have you heard about the CAP theorem?).

b. How many data replicas you will have and what is the impact on the total cost in dollars? Yet another example: what is the average QPS you can serve and the peak load and how it affects the total cost?

c. Is it more convenient to have data in disks, solid state disks or in memory and how this choice can impact the QPS you are able to sustain and the total cost in dollars (Hint: these days storing everything in disk might not be the cheapest solution in terms of money for a given requirement in terms of QPS).

d. What is your storage strategy? Would you adopt a key-value store, a nosql database, a graph database, a SQL database (do you really need a SQL db)?

e. What is you caching strategy? If you have data on disks, can you cache on solid-state disks, can you cache in memory? Again, what about consistency?

f. What is your data partition strategy? Can you provide quicker access to frequently accessed data?

g. Are you running on single machine (most likely no), on a proprietary server farm, or on cloud? What are the implications in terms of latency, throughput and cost?

h. How is your data partitioned in the cloud? Do you have enough network bandwidth? Are you in the same rack or in different racks? Are you in the same data-center or in different data-centers?

i. Do you have a proper production system? What about the test and stage environment? What is the investment you devoted to all the environments in terms of money?

j. Have you considered different use cases for reading data and writing data? Typically, these have different requirements in terms of volume. Again, what about consistency?

k. How do you update data online? Remember that high availability is often a necessary requirement and you cannot afford to have downtime periods. Again, what about consistency?

l. Do you have a compression strategy? What is the impact on costs and performance?

m. How is your networks organized? Do you have proper switches, proxy servers, load balancers, routers, etc

n. Do you have a deployment strategy?

As you start to understand, the list can be expanded forever and you are not supposed to touch all the points in detail. However it is required that you have a good sense of what really matters for your specific problem and you collaborate with the interviewer for deep-diving some well agreed aspects. Again start high level and be more detailed and complex only when required. Please, explain what you are indeed trading off: is it memory, is it disk, is it availability, is it cost, is it time?

3. What are some prerequisites for system interview questions?

Solution

There are many prerequisites for system interview questions such as:

1. Be familiar with quick mathematical estimations. Make sure that you practice calculations with power of 2 and power of 10 (for instance, do you remember what is a petabyte as power of 2 and power of 10?).

2. Be familiar with abstraction concepts. Explain what is exposed and what is hidden by each component. Some elements of object oriented programming can here help.

3. Have a clear sense of what is the different meaning of data storage strategies. Do you know what a relational database is? Do you remember all the different types of joins? When is appropriate NOSQL and when SQL? Are you familiar with scalable key-value stores, and what about graph databases? Have you heard about Mysql, InnoDB, GBDM, Facebook's Cassandra, Hadoop's HBASE, Amazon's Dynamo, Amazon's S3, Google's Map Reduce, Google's BigQuery, Google's Spanner, Google's Borg? If not, it could be useful to check online what they are.

4. Are you familiar with network basics? What is a router, what is a switch, how tcp/ip works, what is DNS, what is a socket, how HTTP works and how HTTP/1.1. works. Again, if you are not familiar it could be useful to check it online.

5. What about concurrency? Do you have a sense of what a process is? and what is the difference with a thread?[1] Are you familiar with synchronization issues?

6. Make sure you are familiar with the CAP theorem and understand the difference among strong, weak and eventual consistency.

7. Make sure you play with some cloud provider infrastructure. For instance, start a number of machines on AWS and write a system that uses all of them.

8. http://highscalability.com has many great articles about how real world systems are designed. It could be always good to understand how they work and learn from them. Another source to consider is https://aphyr.com

4. What are the principles for Web distributed system design?

Solution

Below are some aspects to consider for building web-distributed systems:

---

[1] http://stackoverflow.com/a/809049/832887

- **Availability:** The uptime of a website is critical to the reputation and functionality of web companies. Can you imagine Google stopping to work for a couple of hours? Similar expectations are for small companies as well. Availability requires careful choices for our architectures avoiding single point of failures and introducing replications whenever required. A proper roll-out/deployment infrastructure can also help to increase availability.

- **Consistency:** If data is updated, then future requests for the same object should return the new version data. Can you imagine receiving an email on Gmail and, after a reload, the email is not there yet because you hit a non-updated backend server?

- **Performance:** Website performance is an important factor for web sites. Speed is a key factor for Facebook users' retention; Google search engine's perceived performance, and Twitter newsfeed. Nowadays, fast loading web sites are a common expectation for web users. Amazon found every 100ms of latency cost them 1% in sales[2].

- **Scalability:** Youtube receives 300 hours of videos every minute. Try to guess how the system should scale for supporting that traffic. If you build a system, ask yourself how much additional query traffic it can handle, what is the storage capacity and how it can increase, and how many more transactions can be accepted.

- **Cost:** Money is certainly a key factor. Estimate the cost of hardware, cost of software, and cost of people to develop the system. In addition, take into account how the cost will increase for the next 1-3 years.

---

[2] https://news.ycombinator.com/item?id=273900

5. What is horizontal and vertical scaling?

Solution

"Scaling vertically" means adding more resources to an individual server.
Vertical scaling consists in adding more resources to a server in terms of CPUs, disks, memory, bandwidth, and so on and so forth.

Horizontal scaling consists in adding more computation nodes and it is the most popular way of scaling in the cloud where new nodes can be added on demand.

6. What is sharding?

Solution

Horizontal scaling is typically associated with data partition schema based on shards. Each shards is nothing more than a subset of the whole data obtained using some criteria. Criteria can be based on various attributes extracted from the data and/or on hash functions computed on those attributes. For instance we can partition a repository of Web pages by a hash function on URLs and we can partition a repository of songs by computing a hash function on a suitable songs' signature.

Of course, partition is a tradeoff, which needs to be evaluated in context. If the data is split into multiple pieces, then there might be an issue with data locality. In distributed systems the closer data is to the point of computation, the better system performance is. If that is not the case, we might incur in the need of communications across different computation points. In addition, there could be a problem of inconsistency if different views of the same logical partitions are not synchronized (think about different replica or caching).

7. What are the key requirements while designing a key-value store?

Solution

A key value store has a simple API:

- get(key) – Get the value given a key
- put(key, value) -- Create or update the value given its key
- delete(key) -- Remove the key and the related value

The key-value store runs on a very large number of commoditized machines each of which might have different configuration in terms of CPU, memory and disk. We should assume that at every given instant a number of machines is not available because of failures. Typically a key-value store is implemented by using consistent hashing.

8. What is consistent hashing?

Solution

A simple solution for distributing the keys to S servers is to adopt a hash function such as $H(key) = key \% S$. However, what will happen if a server goes down for a failure? Furthermore, what will happen if a new server needs to be added because we need to increase the storage? In both cases, we need to recompute the hash function on all the keys and redistribute them accordingly. Of course, this is not acceptable.

Consistent Hashing maps all the nodes and the keys in a unit ring. The keys are assigned to the first node encountered walking clockwise on the ring. Note that if a node goes down then we simply need to migrate its keys to the closest node with no need of performing a global reallocation. Likewise, when a new node joins the ring, it can receive (part of) the keys from the adjacent node in anti-clockwise order. Again, the changes are local and not global.

It is possible to further refine the concept by allowing data to be replicated on multiple nodes by simply computing multiple hash functions. In addition, it is possible to distribute the loads if the key distribution is not uniform by representing a computing node with virtual ids which map different points in the unit ring. This can be simply achieved by using multiple hash functions again.

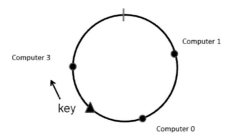

As discussed a node can join and leave the ring at any time. When a new node joins the ring, it will announce its availability to a master directory or via broadcast. As soon as it is recognized, other nodes can migrate their keys according to the model described above. Typically this migration is asynchronous.

Note that there is a number of consistency issues that need to be solved:

1. Some nodes might not have an updated view and keep asking the keywords to the old owners. This problem can be solved by adopting a forward request protocol from the old to the new owner.

2. The new owner can still be in the process of receiving the asynchronous update of its keys. In this case we need a mechanism for determining whether or not the new node is ready to serve the requests. We will discuss this later when we talk about vector clocks.

Furthermore we can keep the updated status of each node by sending periodic heartbeat messages and if a node does not answer for a certain number of intervals, we can consider the node down. Neighbor-nodes will start an asynchronous migration process from one of the replicas of the crashed node. In this way availability is guaranteed and the failed replica is automatically replaced by other alive nodes.

9. What are the different consistency models?

Solution

There are a number of client consistency models:

- Strict Consistency: any write update is observed instantaneously by successive reads.

- Read your write consistency: each client sees its own write update immediately, but not the updates made by other clients.

- Session consistency: same as above, but only for the same session

- Monotonic Read Consistency: the client will only see the same or more updated version of the data in subsequent requests.

- Eventual Consistency: The client can see an inconsistent view when the updates are in progress.

Note that it is not possible to achieve strict consistency and at the same time have data partitioned into multiple replicas. Likewise, eventual consistency is very popular these days because availability is a primary need for many online services.

10. What are the different models of workload distribution?

Solution

There are a number of client consistency models:

- Master-Slave: In this model the master distributes the workload to multiple slaves and it gets their answer. Note that the master can be a single point of failure. Therefore, it could be convenient to have a protocol for electing new masters in case of failures.

- No master: In this model there is no master and the updates are directly sent to multiple replica. Note that it is important to agree on a protocol for guaranteeing that replica achieve some form of consensus on the updated data.

11. What is the CAP Theorem?

Solution

The CAP Theorem states that it is impossible to build a read-write storage that satisfies all of the following three properties:

1. Availability – is the storage system available for read-writes?

2. Consistency - are all executions of reads and writes seen by all nodes as atomic or "linearizably" consistent?

3. Partition tolerance – is the network allowed to drop any messages?

More informally, the CAP theorem states that it is not possible to build a storage system and that both responds to every request and returns consistent results every time.

The key intuition is that if a write request goes to one side of a partition, then any read that goes to the other side of that partition cannot be consistent and it will not give the most recent updates. To put it simple, either the reads have potentially stale information, or they need to wait the other side of the partition to become reachable again.

12. What is 2PC and what is PAXOS?

Solution

2PC

Strict constancy can be implemented by adopting a 2 steps update protocol. During a first step a master sends an update request to multiple servers, which acknowledge the request and write it in a log. During the second step, the master collects all the acknowledgments and then it sends a request of commit to the clients. This 2-step protocol is typically called 2PC. It should be noticed that if one replica is failing, then the master should not send the request to commit during the second stage.

PAXOS

PAXOS is a quorum-based protocol used to achieve consensus among multiple notes. Here, I will present a particular implementation used for Facebook Cassandra[3] and the interested reader can refer Wikipedia for a more complete description of the full class of protocols[4].

For writing, the key idea is to have the master sending the request of N clients and waiting the answer from only $W \leq N$ clients. This is much more efficient from a probabilistic standpoint.

For reading, we need to make sure that the operation reaches at least one replica that has been previously updated successfully. This can be achieved by reading from $R > $ N-W replicas and returning the one with the latest timestamp.

PAXOS is therefore a general framework where it is possible to pick W and R according to the desired workload and the consistency requirements in our application. For instance, when $W = N$ and $R = 1$ we simply have the 2PC protocol. Also strict consistency is achieved when there is an overlap between the write and the read set (e.g. $W + R > N$). Other combinations lead to more relaxed consistency models.

13. What is vector clock?

Solution

Vector clock is a mechanism for generating a partial ordering of events in a distributed system and detecting causality violations. The following steps are followed:

- Initially all clocks are zero;
- Each time a node has an internal event, it increments its own logical clock in the vector by one.

---

[3] https://en.wikipedia.org/wiki/Apache_Cassandra
[4] https://en.wikipedia.org/wiki/Paxos_(computer_science)

- Each time a node sends a message, it attaches the entire vector to the message.
- Each time a node receives a message, it increments its own logical clock and updates each element in its vector by taking the maximum of the value in its own vector clock and the value in the vector in the received message.

Note that each node has always updated information about its internal status. In addition to that, a node will know the status of another node as soon as it gets a message from it. However, the receiver will be informed not only of what is happening to the sending node, but also to all the other nodes that the sending node knows about.

Vector clocks are frequently used for distributing computation and storage. As an example, delete operations can be implemented at logical level where the object appears as "deleted", although they are kept alive long enough time that every replica has very high probability to mark this object as deleted, so the deleted object can be garbage collected at the end.

For the sake of completeness, it could be also useful to mention that there are alternatives to vector clocks. Probably the most common one is the "last-write-wins" where every write includes a timestamp. When conflicts arise then the one with the higher timestamp is selected.

14. What is a Merkle tree?

Solution

A merkle tree is a hash tree where each non-leaf tree is labelled with the hash of the label of its child node. In this way the root has a signature of all the data covered by the tree and recursively each internal node has a signature of subtree it covers.

Ralf Merkle[5] originally patented the idea that is today used for checking data consistency in an incremental way in many distributed storage system.

---

[5] https://en.wikipedia.org/wiki/Ralph_Merkle

15. Design Patterns: What is a pipeline?

Solution

In this pattern a client sends requests to a number of workers connected in sequence. Each module can have an input queue where data flows. For instance, the pattern is frequently used in machine learning for building processing pipelines.

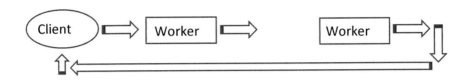

16. Design Patterns: What is a load balancer?

Solution

In this pattern a client sends the request to a dispatcher which selects an available worker from a pool of already known ones. The dispatching policy could be very simple (e.g round robin rotation) or based on an estimation of the less loaded worker. For instance this pattern is used for building scalable web services where the load is partitioned among multiple workers. One open source software load balancer that has received wide adoption is HAProxy[6].

Some load balancers can also route a request differently depending on the type of request (reverse proxies). If a system only has a couple of a nodes, systems like round robin DNS may make more sense since load balancers can be expensive and add an unneeded layer of complexity.

Load balancers can also test the health of a node removing unresponsive nodes and implementing fault-tolerance mechanisms.

---

[6] http://www.haproxy.org/

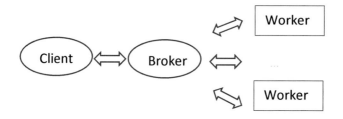

17. Design Patterns: What is a farm of workers?

Solution

In this pattern the dispatcher multicasts a request to all workers in the pool. The computation happens in parallel in all the workers and the results are sent back to the dispatcher which consolidates the answer to all other answers. For instance this pattern is frequently used by search engines to sustain high QPS.

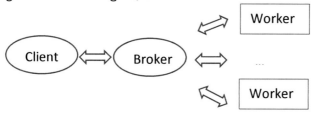

18. Design Patterns: What is a cache?

Solution

In this pattern the dispatcher first checks if the result is already locally available because it has been computed in the past and stored locally. For instance the pattern is very used to achieve high QPS by storing in memory results which need expensive disk access. Memcached[7] and Redis are some commonly used cache servers.

Caches take advantage of temporal locality principle: recently requested data is likely to be requested again. Caches are used in almost every

---

[7] https://memcached.org/

layer from hardware, to operating systems, to web browsers, to web applications. A cache is a short-term memory: it has a limited space, but is typically faster than the original data source and it contains the most recently accessed items.

In a distributed configuration the cache is divided using a consistent hashing function.

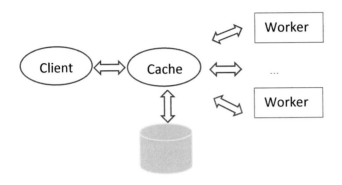

19. Design Patterns: What is a queue?

Solution

A queue is a very simple mechanism to perform asynchronous requests. As a task comes in, it is added to the queue and the worker picks up the next task as soon as it has the capability to process it. Queues are used at all the levels of system design and are an essential element of distributed communications. RabbitMQ[8] is a popular open source solution.

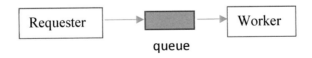

queue

---

[8] https://www.rabbitmq.com/

20. Design Patterns: What is Map and Reduce? An example in spark

Solution

A simple form of parallel computation supported by Spark[9] is the "Map and Reduce" which has been made popular by Google[10] and Hadoop[11]

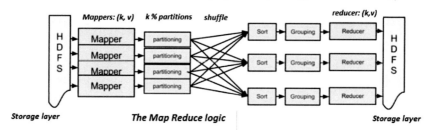

The Map Reduce logic

Mappers receive (key, value) pairs and output (key, value)
Partitioners split the keys into partitions and then shuffle the data
Sorters perform the grouping
Reducers receive (key, iterable[value]) and output (key, value)

In this framework a set of keywords is mapped into a number of workers (e.g. parallel servers available for computation) and the results are then reduced (e.g. collected) by applying a "reduce" operator. The reduce operator could be very simple (for instance a sum) or sophisticated (e.g. a user defined function).

As an example of distributed computation let's compute the Mean Square Error (MSE), the average of the squares of the difference between the estimator and what is estimated. In the following example we suppose that valuesAndPreds is a RDD (e.g. Spark internal representation for distributed data structures) of many $(v_i = $ true labels, $p_i = predictions)$ tuples. Those are mapped into values $(v_i - p_i)^2$. All intermediate results computed by parallel workers are then reduced by applying a sum operator. The final result is then divided by the total number of tuples as defined by the mathematical definition

---

[9] http://spark.apache.org/
[10] http://research.google.com/archive/mapreduce.html
[11] http://hadoop.apache.org/

$$MSE = \frac{1}{n}\sum_{i=1}^{n}(v_i - p_i)^2$$

Spark is a powerful paradigm for parallel computations which are mapped into multiple servers with no need of dealing with low level operations such as scheduling, data partitioning, communication and recovery. Those low level operations were typically exposed to the programmers by previous paradigms. Now Spark solves these problems on our behalf.

Note that Spark hides all the low level details to the programmer by allowing to write a distributed code which is very close to a mathematical formulation. The code uses Python lambda functions.

Code

MSE = valuesAndPreds.map(lambda (v, p): (v - p)**2).reduce(lambda x, y: x + y) / valuesAndPreds.count()

Spark can however support additional forms of parallel computation by taking inspiration from the 20 years of work on skeletons computations and, more recently, on Microsoft's Dryad/Cosmos (which came before Spark).[12]

21.Design Pattern: What is a DAG Scheduler?

Solution

In this pattern the computation is expressed in terms of DAG (direct acyclic graph) where each node is a specific computation piece and edges expresses the computation workflow. A DAG can be seen as a generalization over the two steps (map and reduce) used in Hadoop. In the example below the broker distributes data and sub-tasks of DAG computation to the workers which then elaborate the requests. Note that a mechanism for solving the data and computation dependencies must be implemented.

---

[12] http://codingplayground.blogspot.co.at/2010/09/cosmos-massive-computation-in-microsoft.html

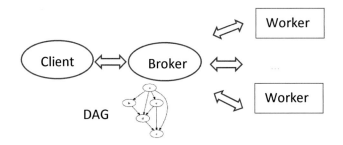

In Spark a driver program interacts with the worker nodes by using the "SparkContext" variable. This interaction is transparent to the user. Each worker node executes assigned tasks and can cache locally the results for computation for future reuse. The results of computations are sent back to the driver program.

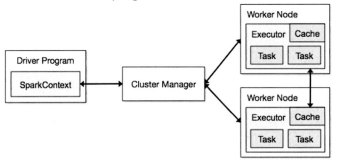

22. Distributed computation: find the top ten visited URLs

Given a large network of computers, each keeping log files of visited URLs, find the top ten of the most visited URLs. The result list must be exact, and the maps are too large to transmit over the network.

Solution

For S servers the exact solution can be achieved in two steps:

1. First step

    a. Ask every server for its own top ten

    b. Merge the results and get the set of top ten from our merge

    c. Pick score of the tenth URL as the threshold T

2. Second step

    a. Ask every server for all its top N with score $\geq T/S$

    b. Merge the results and get the correct top ten

23. Distributed computation: failure

There are S servers and each server is assumed to fail independently with probability p in the time-span of a day, compute the probability of losing at least one server in a day.

Solution

The probability of one not failing is 1-p. The probability of all S not failing will thus be $(1-p)^S$. The probability of at least failing will thus be $1 - (1 - p)^S$. So even if a single server has uptime of 99.95% if we have a very large number of servers (e.g. 10k) the probability of a failure among one of them is very high (99.3%).

24. Distributed computation: generating a unique ID

Design a system to return a unique ID for each request.

Solution

A naïve solution is to generate an ID as a function of the timestamp. However, this solution has two problems. First, what if we need to address a very high QPS and generate those IDs with a distributed system? In this case, multiple independent servers can generate the same ID. Second, even with a single server what will happen if the rates of requests is higher that the granularity of the timestamp? In this case, the same ID will be generated for two consecutive requests. Both problems are violating the requirements of our system.

A more sophisticated solution is to generate the IDs by combining timestamps, with information related to the server such as system unique ID or MAC addresses.

Furthermore, in order to solve the problems of request's rates higher than the timestamp granularity we can pre-generate a number of IDs and store them in memory.

This strategy works well in any classical consumer-producer problem. Creating a pool of pre-allocated objects can mitigate the problem of running out as consumers request them.

25. Distributed computations: design an elevator system

How would you optimize an elevator system for a building with 50 floors and 4 elevators? Optimize in terms of lowest wait times for the users.

Solution

A first intuition is to distribute the elevators in different floors so that they are close enough to the customers. We have 50 floors and 4 elevators so the first elevator goes to the ground floor, the second one to the 13th floor, the third one to the 25th, the fourth one to the 38th floor. These floors are the base positions when there are no outstanding requests. Each elevator will return to the base positions which are not already occupied by other elevators.

Furthermore, we can keep a direction of movement until we arrive to the very ground floor or to the roof. In other words, if an elevator goes up (or down), it keeps going until there are pending requests for that directions. This strategy can be implemented by using two queues (one up and one down).

Additional strategies can be put in place. For instance we can consider that in the morning the users tends to go up and in the afternoon they tend to go down (because they are supposed to leave the building). Also, we can consider that certain floors can get more traffic than others (e.g. ground floor or cafeteria). Pre-allocating elevators to the appropriate floors can be useful in such cases.

26. Distributed computation: design a rate limiting system

Solution

The system has throttled the number of requests received. A standard algorithm for this problem is called token bucket/leaky. Each client has a bucket containing a number of tokens. Each time a new action has to be performed, a token is removed from the bucket, and if no tokens are available, then the user is put on hold. The bucket is refilled according to the rate limit. Note that each refill operation needs a write and each removal of a token is a write. Essentially, we need a $long$ (or a $long$ $long$) for each client. Writing all the times can be very expensive and does not scale with the number of users.

An alternative is to have a timestamp associated to the bucket that is updated at each refill interval. When a client needs to access the resource, it will check the timestamp and calculate the number of requests that should have been performed since the last epoch. If this number exceeds the requested rate then the operation is not performed.

Projects

27.Project: Design a photo hosting system

Solution

This problem is generic enough and the solutions adopted for scalability, data, and design can be therefore utilized in other contexts too.

Requirements

Let us start from a high-level definition of what are the requirements. We can assume that our system has an increasing number of U users and an increasing number of P pictures. Users can post, delete and view pictures. A user can follow other users. Under these assumptions, we need to model a picture object and a user object and to express the relations user-user and user-picture.

Note that the set of requirements defined here are by choice very basics and can be extended in multiple ways. A modern photo hosting system has certainly additional features. For instance photos can be commented and tagged (think about Flickr). Furthermore, images can be searched either by tag, by comments and more generally by metadata fields (think about Google Photo). Images can also be browsed with the so-called 'timeline' feature (think about your personalized images stream posted by your friends in Instagram). In addition to that, it should be possible to define access policies so that certain users should not be allowed to access specific (sets of) images (think about Facebook's privacy settings). Besides, images can be stored in multiple formats ranging from raw formats to compressed images to various types of thumbnails and these types of conversions should frequently happen in a transparent way for the user (think about Google Photo). Additionally, images can be synched across multiple devices again in ways that should be transparent to the user (a very popular feature these days among Google, Amazon, Dropbox, Microsoft, and many additional cloud providers).

High level design

Now, suppose that the interviewer will ask you to focus on image posting, reading and deleting. You can start by drawing a high-level functional schema on the whiteboard similar to one reported below

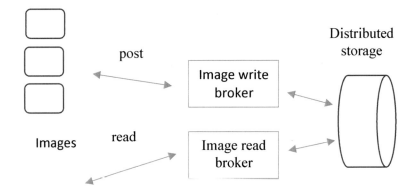

In a Service-Oriented Architecture (SOA), each service has its own distinct functional role and offers functionalities through a well-defined API. The advantages of SOA are in terms agility, scalability, and maintenance. For instance, we decided to separate reads from writes even in our high-level view because it is appropriate to assume that those two operations have different needs in terms of operations per second. In addition, reads can be asynchronous while writes are typically synchronous.

While drawing the high-level design you might mention that, you would expect 10x more reads than writes (think about Instagram) and that you need a distributed storage perhaps with few optimizations such as compression, in-memory caching, and edge caching services such as Akamai[13]. At this stage do not go in too many deep details but pay attention to feedback provided by the interviewer and if it is worth expanding those points later on.

Storage

The storage system can be based on a distributed key-value store based on consistent hashing. We need a table 'Picture' where the key is a unique id associated to the picture and the value is the raw image data. We also need to add another table 'Metadata' where the key is their picture id and the value consists of a combination of picture specific metadata (e.g. quality of the photo, geolocation, etc) and user generated metadata (tagging, likes). We also need a table 'UserPicture' where the key is a unique id associated to each user and the value is a

---

[13] https://www.akamai.com/

list of all pictures (s)he owns. Furthermore, we need a table 'UserUser' to store the relations among users. Note that the distributed key-value store offers reliability using k replica for each information stored. Deletes are typically logical with the space freed after d days for supporting undeletes. Updates are typically in append mode with data attached to the values for each key. Obviously, we use an already available data store such as Cassandra[14].

Note that a key-value store is not the only choice: we can adopt a range of solutions ranging from NOSQL (with no support for relational joins) to SQL (with support for relational joins). Facebook for instance started with a storage layer for images based MYSQL, Nettapp over NFS using SATA drivers with in-memory and in-SSD disks caching.[15] In this solution, scalability can be addressed by distributing users across different shards so that each shard serves a set number of users and as users increase more shards are added to the cluster. Sharding can also be applied to the pictures if required.

Note that all those choices have implications and tradeoffs. For instance sharding for instance is good for scalability but might require more communications to access information located in different shards. Storage in SSD can be more expensive but generally offers higher QPS. Make sure that you discuss those implications with the interviewer. Again, remember that (s)he is also trying to understand your communication skills and whether or not you can be a good fit for the team.

Redundancy & Availability

Redundancy must be supported at all levels in our system. We already have seen some redundancy mechanism for storage. However, we should pay attention to single points for failure in our design. For instance, in our high-level design for photo hosting both the image posting and the reading brokers are single point of failure. If they go down all the system will be un-accessible. That is not good so we need to think about replication mechanisms at this level too. The most

---

[14] https://en.wikipedia.org/wiki/Apache_Cassandra
[15]

http://www.enterprisestorageforum.com/sans/features/article.php/3797646/Facebook-Friends-Storage-Vendors.htm

scalable solution is a share-nothing architecture where no single broker needs to talk with other brokers for concluding its jobs.

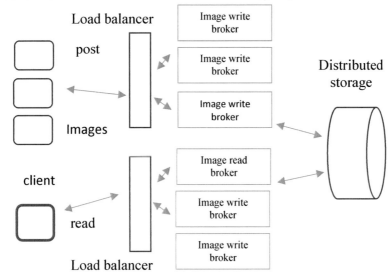

In addition, it could be convenient to have essentially stateless brokers so that they be replaced when needed. If we need to implement a session state this can be achieved with client-side mechanisms such as cookies. Different brokers can be balanced via DNS round robin[16] and/or with ad-hoc solutions such as F5[17]. Apart from that, brokers and storage can run on commodity servers.

28.Project: Design a distributed cache

Solution

Designing a cache system in a single server requires a way to keep a list of objects to be deleted via a garbage collection policy. In addition, it requires a way to access each object in $O(1)$.

Requirements

a) Store an object in cache

b) Retrieve an object from cache

---

[16] https://en.wikipedia.org/wiki/Round-robin_DNS
[17] https://f5.com/

Besides we need to implement a mechanism for garbage collection that is triggered when the cache runs out of space. Furthermore, we might want to implement additional methods for usage statistics.

High level design

Implementing a cache on a distributed system is a typical design problem with consistency and availability issues. A cache can be:

- Local: each server holds a particular sub-set of the full key space.

- Global: each server holds a particular sub-set of the full key space but the access is seamless for the client that is not aware of the partition.

In both cases, solutions for availability should be in place with a number of suitable server replicas. At the same time, solutions for data consistency among the cache nodes should be available. A distributed cache is frequently implemented by using consistent hashing[18].

Coding

This is a skeleton of the code for a single server implementation. The LRU cache has a map from string to `CacheEntry`. Besides, it holds a pointer to the list of objects that can be garbage collected. Every time a cache entry is accessed in the map it must be also moved to the front of the list. In this implementation each `CacheEntry` also stores a key for $O(1)$ removals.

```
class CacheEntry{
    private cacheEntry next, prev;
    private string key, value;

    . . .
}

class LRUCache{

    private map<string, cacheEntry> map; // hold the
cacheEntries
```

---

[18] http://dl.acm.org/citation.cfm?id=313019

```
    private CacheEntry head, tail;          // hold the
list for GC
    private long maxSize;                    // maxSize


    . . .
}
```

29. Project: Design a Tiny URL

Solution

Designing a tiny URL system is a popular question because it addresses topics according to many aspects of the system design interview.

Requirements

a) Shortening: given a long URL, encode it in a short URL with a fixed length.
b) Decoding: given a short URL provided as a string, return the correspondent long URL.

For instance,
http://www.enterprisestorageforum.com/sans/features/article.php/3797646/F acebook-Friends-Storage-Vendors.htm could be encoded into
http://tinyurl.com/abYX23 by using an appropriate bijective function.

Estimating the size of the problem

Suppose that you need to estimate the number of URLs submitted to the service every day. One approach is to use some other well-known metric and approximate the answer. Note that the above numbers are an approximation and what really matters is the ballpark estimation and the consistency in our methodology.

Twitter has 400M posts per day and it is an important source for short URLs. Suppose that 50% of those posts contains a short url →200M and that our system get 5% of this traffic → 10M/day → 70M/week ; assume that some additional traffic will come from external sources and round it to 100M/week. Furthermore, suppose that redirects are 10x more than the submitted URLs. For instance, this can be justified assuming that a tweet post will be clicked 10 times → 1 billion redirects/week. We can therefore estimate the average QPS for redirects as $10^9/(7*87*10^3)$ = $(10*10^8)/(6*10^6)$ = 166QPS. However, it is safe to assume at least 400QPS peak.

In addition to that, let us assume that shortened URLs are made up of 6 characters and that original URLs are made of 255 characters. For sake of simplicity let us also assume that each character is one byte (Unicode will only increase the size).

High level design

For converting from long to short URL the steps are:
1. Save URL in a database
2. Get a unique ID for that URL from database
3. Convert integer ID to short string with an encode function. Then if we assume that the URL is
4. Use the short string in our short URLs

Vice versa, for converting from short to long URL the steps are:

5. Covert the short URL string into an unique ID with decode()
6. Return the original long string given the unique ID

Note that I have preferred to use a unique ID instead of directly hashing each long URL. This is for avoiding potential collisions between two URLS.

We can use a consistent hashing key-value store for maintaining the association between unique ID and long URLs (note that we also need the inverse relation). Furthermore, we need to generate a new ID for each new unseen long URL.

A SOA based infrastructure with no single point of failure can also help to address scalability and availability in a way similar to what has been done for the design of photo systems. For the sake of brevity that considerations are not reported here.

Coding

If required, you can sketch a code fragment for encoding and decoding:

```
private static final String CHAR_MAP =
"abcdefghijklmnopqrstuvwxyzABCDEFGHIJKLMNOPQRSTUVWXYZ012345
6789";
private static final int BASE = CHAR_MAP.length();

private static String idToShortURL(int id) {

    StringBuilder sb = new StringBuilder();

    while(id > 0) {
        sb.append(CHAR_MAP.charAt(id%BASE));
        id = id / BASE;
    }
    return sb.reverse().toString();
}

private static int shortURLtoID(String shortUrl) {
    int no = 0;
    for(char c : shortUrl.toCharArray()) {
        no = no * BASE + CHAR_MAP.indexOf(c);
    }
        return no;
}

//tests - main method
public static void main(String args[]) {

    String shortUrl = idToShortURL(1234);
    System.out.println("shortUrl : " + shortUrl);
    System.out.println("ID : " +
shortURLtoID(shortUrl));

}
```

30. Project: Design a Web search engine

Solution

This is another popular system design interview question. I like this question because the interviewer has the opportunity to understand your abstraction and communication skills and can ask to go deep on specific aspects. No one can really build a search engine in one hour interview, so make sure that you focus only on the specific aspects required by the interviewer.

Requirements

Left as an exercise

High level design

A Web search engine starts with a collection of Web documents. There are four main components: a crawler, and indexer, a query engine, and a ranker. The crawler collects the corpus of data, while the indexer allows identifying which documents contain specific words (in a way similar to the analytical index contained at the end of many books). The crawler needs to avoid infinite loops when it follows web links. Furthermore, it needs to avoid hammering target web sites with a huge number of requests in a short amount. The indexer is typically built with a map-reduce (left as an exercise) on a massive cluster of parallel servers.

Additional meta-information can also be built. For instance, we might need to compute a pagerank score again using map-reduce[19], or we might need to aggregate users' clicks collected in the past to improve the ranking of the search results. Furthermore, we could process the crawled text for tagging a specific part-of-speech.

Once the index is built, it should be sharded into multiple servers for sustaining the search QPS (google is estimated to have 40K QPS). Multiple solutions can be adopted: should you partition by keywords, or should you partition buy documents? Moreover, what are the implications for both choices. Equally important do not forget to think about availability and how to address failures.

The query engine will parse the users' queries and access the index for finding the documents containing them. The retrieved documents are then ordered so that the most relevant documents are returned as top results. A relevance engine is typically made by two components: a ranker based on query-independent signals only based on documents (e.g. PageRank); and a ranker which also considers query signals. More in general, ranking should at least take into account three different classes of signals: textual relevance, link based relevance, and user feedback based relevance.

The discussion can be expanded in multiple directions but make sure that you consider the scalability aspects. A good starting point is to

---

[19] http://michaelnielsen.org/blog/using-mapreduce-to-compute-pagerank/

estimate the size of the document repository and its cost in terms of money.

Estimating the size of the problem

Let us suppose that the size of the web is 1T web pages (10^{12}). Furthermore, let us suppose that each page is 10Kbytes with 1K words each. The size is reduced after compression to 2Kbytes (compression ratio 80%). In addition, let us assume that there are 3 data replica and 5 data versions. Let us expect that each server have 24TB disk, 1Tb SSDs and 256Gb memory.

Google claimed 40K/second queries in 2012 [40K*87Kday =3500M =3,5B/day] on 10 datacenters which is 4K/sec per datacenter, say with peak at 12K/sec.

Storage

Given those assumptions, we can estimate the number of servers for data needed for a data repository [with no index, and only one data version] as Total space = #pages X size X replica = 1T*2K*3= 6K*1T= 6000*1Tbytes.

31. If the data is stored on disks, we get that the number of servers is 6000/24T=250 for storing all the documents. Each server gets 1T/250 = 4 billion docs. The cost in terms of money is 250*$3K=750K$. However, we need data replica for sustaining QPS. Assuming that each cluster has 100QPS then we need 120x$750K=$90M, since we have 12k QPS/100QPS ;

32. If data is stored on SSD disks, we get that the number of servers is 6000/8T = 750 (with an increase 3x considering the above solution) for storing all the documents. Each server gets 1T/740 = 1.3billion documents. The cost in terms of money is 750*6K=$4,5M. However, SSD allows having a higher QPS (say 10x). Therefore, assuming each cluster has 1000QPS, then we need 12x$4,5M=$54M;

33. If the data is stored in memory, we get that the number of servers is 6000/0.256= 24K servers. The cost in terms of money is 24K * 3K$ = 72M$. Each server gets $10*10^{11}/2,4*10^4=4,1*10^8=410M$ docs (2^{31} unique ids). Note that it can easily get to 15Kqps on a single server if the repository is in memory

Web index

An index can be used like a table of contents that guides you to the location where your data exists. In the index, each word is associated with a list of documents containing the word (this representation is called inverted indexes). These indexes are often stored in memory and organized in hierarchies. Indeed, it might be convenient to have many layers of indexes that serve as a map, moving from one location to the next, until you get the specific piece of data you want. Creating intermediate indexes and representing the data in smaller slices makes big data problems controllable. Data can be spread across many servers and still accessed quickly. Each document has a unique ID represented as long.

In our examples, each server has ~410M docs requiring 32 bit for representing the document with no compression. Variable length encoding compressions are used on list of integers to save space. Overall, we can estimate a need of an additional 25%-40% additional space with an increase in terms of cost.

34. Project: Design a YouTube repository

Solution

This problem is left as an exercise. However, let us concentrate on one only aspect:

Estimating the size of the problem

In 2015 Youtube claimed that there are 300 hours of videos submitted every minute. Therefore assuming an encoding of 20Kbit/sec, we get that 1 hour is 20Kbit/sec*3600sec = $20*10^3*3,6*10^3$bit = 72Mbit=9Mb. Therefore 300hours are 300*9mb=2,7Gb each minute (approximatively 3Gb each min). Therefore, for every hour we need an additional 60*3Gb=180Gb. This means that every day we need 24 * 180Gb = 4,4T, and every year 365*4,4TB=1,6Pb of disk.

However, this is not enough because we certainly need to keep various encodings for different video formats (say 4), and multiple replica (say

3) for availability. Furthermore, we need to keep the previous years and we assume a model of growth 50% YoY. Previous 2 years are similar to the current one. Previous 4 years are similar to current one. So 6 past years are 6Pb disks. In addition to this, we need to plan the growth for the next year. In total, we have 4 video formats * 3 replica * (6 + 2 + 4) PB = 144 PB needed to store the videos

In addition, we need to keep video thumbnails (which are many small files), we need to store an index, evaluate the required QPS, and estimate the cost in terms of money for the whole system.

35.Project: Design a Facebook style news feed

Solution

Requirements

Left as an exercise, assuming that the reader uses at least one social network.

High level design

Left as an exercise. However, it could be interesting to read what Andrew Boz the inventor of Facebook newsfeed posted on quora[20]. His posting is a great example of how simple solutions are usually the most effective.

Boz wrote: "*I appreciate how far the web has come in the past several years that all the discussion around this topic considers only real time solutions. The original version of News Feed on Facebook, which was up for over two years before being replaced, actually wasn't real time. We swept through all the users about every 15 or 30 minutes and wrote the new stories to MySQL in large updates. We would publish stories at 5*

---

[20] https://www.quora.com/What-are-the-best-practices-for-building-something-like-a-News-Feed

minute intervals into the future to give the appearance of a steady stream of information. ... If I log in once a day and want to see the best stories, I think most developers would be better off spending time working on the relevance than the delivery."

Therefore, Boz suggests pre-computing the feeds offline and that solutions scaled well for all the first two years in Facebook. If you really need to have real-time feeds than there are two possible scenarios.

Push Model

Data is de-normalized and pushed to all the users' friends in real-time. Obviously, the content is not pushed but only metadata and pointers to data repositories. The problem with this solution is that many friends are updated even if they are not always logged in. This means that we will have many writes for data that we potentially not accessed. It could be convenient to store the data in open sources repositories such as Cassandra[21], which is nowadays used by Facebook. Another solution is to use MySQL[22] perhaps with a layer of in-memory cache such as memcached[23] (this was the solution adopted by Facebook for years) or Redis[24] (this is the solution adopted by Twitter).

Pull Model

All the recent activity is cached in memory and retrieved whenever users load their feed. The problem with this solution is that we can have immediate burst of communications with unpredictable patterns among our nodes in the clusters. As an exercise, the reader could think about data partition strategies for sharding the data in such a way that the

---

[21] http://cassandra.apache.org/
[22] https://www.mysql.com/
[23] https://memcached.org/
[24] http://redis.io/

communication latencies are minimized. As an additional note, we can adopt a storage strategy like the one described above.

High level design

I will omit this one because it is similar to previous discussion.

Estimating the size of the problem

Left an exercise.

Ranking

Ranking should at least take into account four different classes of signals: affinity score with the friend, a score for the friend, a textual score for the content posted, and a temporal decay score.

Scalability

Facebook has 1.6 billion users and scalability is achieved through data sharding, in-memory caching, massive adoption of commodity servers and load balancers. Considerations similar to what already said for the Image Photo system hold.

36. Project: Design a Whatsup Messaging Service

Solution

Requirements

a) Contact list: we need to maintain a list of contacts together with their state (online, offline, away)
b) Asynchronous messages: we need to maintain a queue of pending messages that are delivered when the user is online.

High level design

Left an exercise. We need a server for maintaining the contact list and a server for delivering asynchronous messages. The former has to maintain a connection open with each client that pushes status information. This status information is then broadcasted to the appropriate clients. The latter can be based on either push or pull mechanism in a way similar to the Facebook design. Pay attention to scalability issues, data partition/sharing and caching opportunities.

Estimating the size of the problem

Left an exercise.

37. Project: Design an in-memory cache similar to Memcached

Solution

Requirements

a)   Store a key-value entry, if there is still available space
b)   Retrieve a value given a key
c)   Delete a value given a key (logical delete)
d)   Free space when needed.

High level design

Left an exercise. However, some key elements are reported here. First, we can use a key-value store based on consistent hashing. At the very beginning, it could be useful to pre-allocate a memory pool for incoming requests. Those are served by using one bucket from the pool (use locks when needed to avoid problems with concurrency). In addition, we need to implement a Least Recent Used (LRU) policy for garbage collection when the space is almost ended. Furthermore, we need to implement a distributed lock for keeping objects into a LRU list. Deleted entries can be market for logical deletion.

Estimating the size of the problem

Left an exercise. It could be useful to estimate the cost per terabyte.

38. Project: Design an Auto-complete system

Solution

Requirements

a)   Store previous queries generated from users together with clicks. This information is used for generating suggestions offline

b) A frontend system, which queries the backend for each character entered by the user into the searchbox.
c) A backend system which given a query prefix (e.g "pit") retrieves the most likely suggestions ("e.g. "pitbul").

High level design

The logging system has to capture previous queries submitted to the search query box and clicks for selecting suggestions.

The frontend system is typically implemented in AJAX, with requests sent asynchronously to the backend for each character entered by the user in the search box.

The backend has to return the most likely suggestions for each query prefix. One simple and scalable solution is to store each prefix into a key-value store where the values are the suggestions associated to the prefix. The association between prefixes and suggestions can be computed offline by using the information stored by the logging system.

Other solutions can be adopted based on Tries[25] or Ternary trees[26] but those might be more difficult to scale into a distributed system. As an exercise, think what could mean to shard a trie into multiple partitions.

Caching can be adopted at multiple levels for reducing the amount of communications between the client and the frontend and between the frontend and the backend.

Estimating the size of the problem

Left an exercise.

_____

[25] https://en.wikipedia.org/wiki/Trie
[26] https://en.wikipedia.org/wiki/Ternary_tree

39. Project: Design a Recommendation System

Solution

Requirements

Given a list of movies (or songs or academic papers) recommend the one to watch for a user

High level design

Recommender systems produce a list of recommendations such as news to read, movies to see, music to listen, research articles to read, books to buy and so on and so forth. The recommendations are generated through two main approaches that are often combined:

- **Collaborative filtering** aims to learn a model from a user's past behaviour (items previously purchased or clicked and/or numerical ratings attributed to those items) as well as similar choices made by other users. The learned model is then used to predict items (or ratings for items) that the user may have an interest in. Note that in some situations rating and choices can be explicitly made, while in other situations those are implicitly inferred by users' actions. Collaborative filtering has two variants:

  - **User-based collaborative filtering: the** user's interest is taken into account by looking for users who are somehow similar to him/her. Each user is represented by a profile and different kinds of similarity metrics can be defined. For instance a user can be represented by a vector and the similarity could be the cosine similarity
  - **Item-based collaborative filtering: the** user's interest is directly taken into account by aggregating similar classes of interest

- **Content-based filtering** aims to learn a model based on a series of features related to an item in order to recommend additional items with similar properties. For instance, a content based filtering system can recommend an article similar to other articles seen in the past, or it can recommend a song with a sound similar to ones implicitly liked in the past.

Recommenders have generally to deal with a bootstrap problem for suggesting recommendations to new unseen users for whom very few information about their tastes are available. In this case, a solution could be to cluster new users according to different criteria such us gender, age, location and/or to leverage a complete set of signals such as time of the day, day of the week, etc. One easy approach is to recommend what is popular, where the definition of popularity could be either global or conditioned to a few and simple criteria.

More sophisticate recommenders can also leverage additional structural information. For instance, an item can be referred by other items and those can contribute to enrich the set of features. As an example, think about a scientific publication that is referred to by other scientific publications. In this case, the citation graph is a very useful source of information for recommendations.

We leave the reader the task for discussing the details in architecture. However, it could be useful to suggest some high level modules that could be considered

1. **User profile builder:** used to build and maintain a profile for each user;

2. **Recommendation Core:** used to generate recommendations;

3. **Filtering:** used to filter recommendations already seen by the user;

4. **Ranking:** used to rank recommendations by taking into account multiple factors such as relevance for the user, freshness and others.

5. **Feedback Analyzer:** used to store the feedback provided by the user, either explicitly or implicitly.

Estimating the size of the problem

Left as an exercise.

ABOUT THE AUTHOR

An experienced data mining engineer, passionate about technology and innovation in consumers' space. Interested in search and machine learning on massive dataset with a particular focus on query analysis, suggestions, entities, personalization, freshness and universal ranking. Antonio Gullì has worked in small startups, medium (Ask.com, Tiscali) and large corporations (Microsoft, RELX). His carrier path is about mixing industry with academic experience.

Antonio holds a Master Degree in Computer Science and a Master Degree in Engineering, and a Ph.D. in Computer Science. He founded two startups, one of them was one of the earliest search engine in Europe back in 1998. He filed more than 20 patents in search, machine learning and distributed system. Antonio wrote several books on algorithms and currently he serves as (Senior) Program Committee member in many international conferences. Antonio teaches also computer science and video game programming to hundreds of youngsters on a voluntary basis.

"Nowadays, you must have a great combination of research skills and a just-get-it-done attitude."

Made in the USA
San Bernardino, CA
19 July 2017